PURR!

A Children's Book About Cats

Written by
Andrea M. Nelson-Royes
and Natalie A. Royes

Art by
Jerry Craft

Written by Andrea M. Nelson-Royes and Natalie A. Royes

Illustrated and designed by Jerry Craft

Edited by Bobbie Christmas

Text copyright ©2015 by Andrea M. Nelson-Royes

Cover art and illustrations ©2015 by Jerry Craft

ISBN-13: 978-0692699041
ISBN-10: 069269904X

All rights reserved. No part of this book may be reproduced, or stored in a retrieval system, or transmitted in any form by any means electronic or mechanical, including photocopying, recording or otherwise, without prior written permission, except in the case of brief quotations embodied in critical articles and reviews.

Library of Congress Control Number: 2016907034

This book is dedicated to
Our Family,
whose love and
encouragement inspire
us.

TABLE OF CONTENTS

- ABOUT CATS
- KITTENS
- FINDING A CAT
- BRINGING YOUR CAT HOME
- FOOD
- WATER
- TOYS
- LITTER BOX
- GROOMING
- EMOTIONS
- VET
- NEUTERING OR SPAYING
- DECLAWING
- FIVE POPULAR BREEDS OF CATS
- CONCLUSION
- GLOSSARY / INDEX
- WEBSITES
- ABOUT THE AUTHORS

ABOUT CATS

Most *domestic cats*, or *house cats*, are friendly, smart, loving, and playful. Cats are sometimes called *felines or mousers*. They are great pets for most children and adults. Cats are mammals, which are animals that nourish their young with milk and are warm-blooded.

Warm-blooded animals keep a healthy body temperature without the help of an outside source of warmth.

They have beautiful eyes that see well in the dark.

Most cats have fur or hair on their bodies. On their faces, they have long hairs called whiskers.

whiskers

A cat's sense of smell is 14 times stronger than that of a human being.
Cats also have good hearing and can hear sounds far away.

Feline tails have many muscles. The animals use these muscles to balance or as a means of expression. A cat uses its tail to express curiosity, happiness, and anger.

Cats like to sleep. They sleep 16 to 18 hours a day. The slightest noise can wake them up. In the wild, being alert keeps wild cats from falling prey to predators.

Wild cats chase other animals and eat them for food. House cats are not wild animals. Lions, tigers, leopards, and other wild cats are also related to domestic cats.

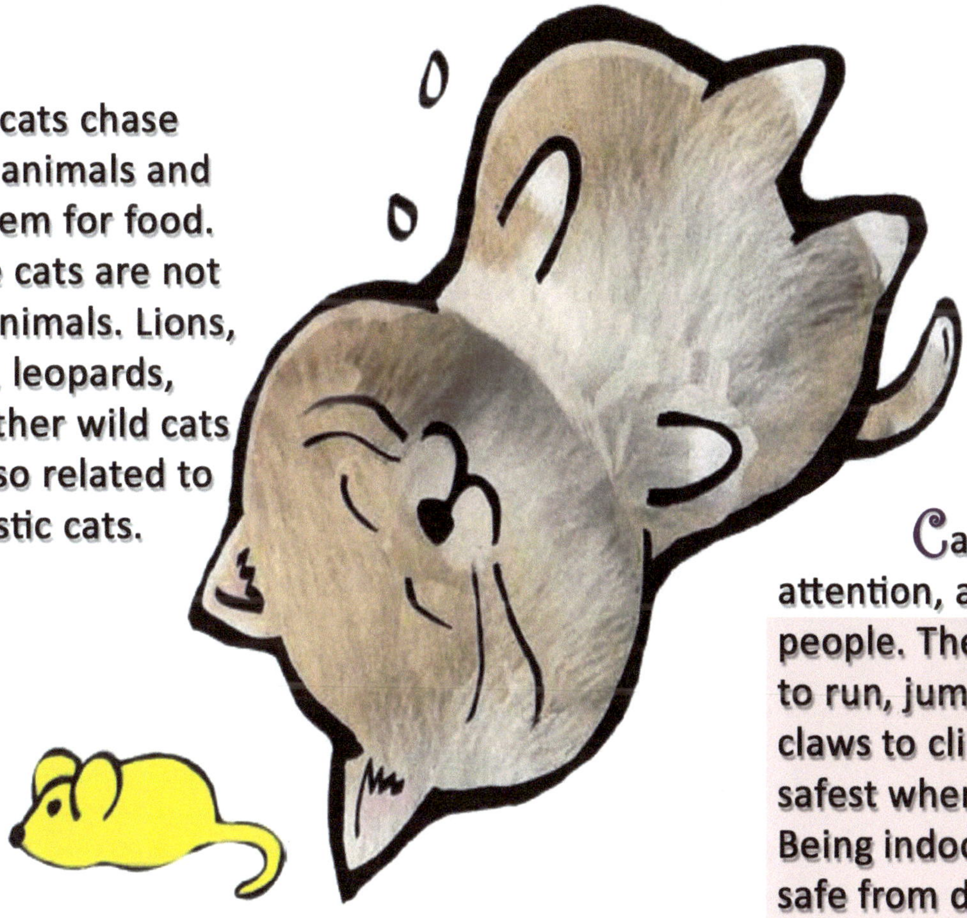

Cats need love, attention, and care from people. These mousers like to run, jump, and use their claws to climb. Cats are safest when kept indoors. Being indoors keeps them safe from dogs, cars, and other danger.

KITTENS

Kittens are baby cats, they are small, furry, and soft. Newborn kittens are tiny and weak. Baby cats are helpless and sleep most of the time. Kittens cannot open their eyes or hear until they are about two weeks old; therefore, kittens should not leave their mother until they are about two to three months old. After about three weeks, felines grow strong enough to walk around.

Kittens get teeth when they are one month old. Baby cats are playful and like to run. They are considered adult cats when they are one year old.

A one year old cat has about the same maturity as a twenty-four-year old person.

After one year, cats age about four years for every human year.

Cat Glasses

Healthy cats can live up to twenty years. The oldest cat on record lived to be thirty-six years old.

Are you ready to be a friend to your cat his whole life? Let's read on.

FINDING A CAT

An animal shelter in your local community is one place to find a cat. An animal shelter is a center that cares for animals that do not have homes. You can also buy a cat at a pet store, or ask friends if they know of anyone who has a cat with kittens. The cat owner might be giving the kittens away.

Choose a cat or kitten that has good muscle tone and bright, clear eyes. The animal must also be alert and friendly.

BRINGING YOUR CAT HOME

The following is a list of the basic pet supplies you will need when you bring home a cat or kitten:

Pet carrier
Food and water dishes
Cat or kitten food
Litter box
Cat litter
Litter scoop
Cat bed
Scratching post
Cat toys
Grooming supplies

A cat may hide when you bring him home, because he feels uneasy. Do not pull your cat from his hiding place. He will come to you when he is ready.

FOOD

Indoor cats depend on people for food. They need food daily. Cats should have a special food bowl. After every meal, wash your cat's food bowl with warm, soapy water, and rinse it clean. Cats need to be fed two times a day. Kittens need to be fed three or four times a day. It is best to keep your cat on a fixed feeding schedule.

Cats like their food at room temperature. Their food must be high-quality and protein-rich, unless your veterinarian suggests another food for health reasons. Their food must contain the right mixture of nutrients for a balanced diet. A balanced diet allows cats to live and grow. It also keeps them healthy. Cats can eat wet or dry food.

Some foods are bad for cats. Do not give your cat foods such as milk, chocolate, or avocadoes. Some cats cannot digest these foods, and they can get an upset stomach. These foods can also cause vomiting and diarrhea.

WATER

Indoor cats also depend on people for water. Cats need plenty of clean water to drink. Cats should have a special water bowl. Each time your cat is given dry food, he will need to get more water.

If he does not get enough water, he will get sick from thirst. Rinse and refill your cat's water bowl at least twice a day, because cats will not drink dirty water.

Cats avoid water that has a foul smell or taste.

Toys

Apart from food and water, cats need lots of toys to play with. Keep a box of cat toys where your cat can see them. Choose toys that are safe and fun. Cats like simple toys such as balls, sticks, strings, straws, and fake mice. Sometimes a paper grocery bag, a shoebox, or a piece of rolled-up paper will keep your cat amused. Catnip or cat grass can make your cat excited and more playful than usual.

Because cats like to climb and jump, try a cat tree with a scratching post. A scratching post can keep your cat from scratching the furniture.

To keep the house safe for cats, pick up small objects or toys that your cat could swallow or choke on. These items include small pieces of plastic, rubber bands, scraps of strings, wire bread-wrapper ties, paperclips, buttons, bows, or hairpins.

LITTER BOX

Most cats know to go to the bathroom in a litter box without being shown. Kittens learn by watching their mothers. If your kitten has not yet learned to use a litter box, you will have to show him. Put him in the litter box when he wakes up from sleeping or a few times during the day. Soon he will learn that the litter box is where he should go to the bathroom.

Cats depend on people to keep their litter box clean. If the litter box is not clean, your cat can get sick or use somewhere else in the house as a bathroom. A cat's litter box needs to be spacious and in a quiet place away from his food area.

Scoop your cat's litter box at least once a day or as often as possible after use. Unless you use a special flushable litter, put the soiled litter in a bag and place it in a trash can. The litter box must be changed completely at least once a week. Wash the litter box with warm, soapy water. Dry the litter box before pouring in new litter.

Remember to wash your hands with warm, soapy water afterwards.

GROOMING

Most cats do not like to bathe in water. Instead cats like to groom themselves. In fact, they spend about 30% of their time each day grooming. They lick their fur, chew their claws, and rub their paws over their face, to clean themselves.

Cats swallow hair when they lick their fur, though. Swallowing too much hair can cause lumps of hair, or hairballs, to form in their stomachs. Hairballs make kitties vomit, so brush your cat often to avoid them.

There are special brushes for cats, so choose a good one. If your cat has short hair, brush him once a week. If your cat has long hair, brush him every day. Most cats enjoy being brushed, because they like the attention.

PURRRRR

EMOTIONS

Cats are very emotional pets. They may pick up on, and match, their owner's mood. Try to keep your cat in a happy and cheerful mood. If your cat exposes his stomach to you, he feels safe and secure around you. Cats may become aggressive or sad if they do not get enough attention from their owners.

Playing with your cat everyday keeps him happy and is good exercise. Cats need exercise to stay healthy. Some cats may bite, usually gently, when they are happy.

Kitty cats may do things you do not want them to do. Your cat might jump on the kitchen counter or dinner table. If so, take him off and say, "**No**." Never hit, yell, or hurt your cat. Hitting, yelling, or hurting your cat will teach him to be afraid of you. Sometimes squirting a little water from a spray bottle, or speaking sternly to your cat, will help him know when he has done something wrong. Always be gentle, so the cat will trust you and be more likely to listen.

Tabbies can meow for many reasons. They may feel insecure, hungry, or need your attention. As a cat owner, you should learn your cat's emotions and respond accordingly.

VET

𝒜 veterinarian (vet) is a medical doctor who treats animals. Within the first week of getting your cat, bring him or her to the vet for a checkup. The vet will make sure your cat has all of his shots and is healthy. Even if your cat is in good health, you need to take him to the vet once or twice a year for a checkup. A physical examination twice a year prevents most major cat diseases such as diabetes, obesity, and bone and joint disease.

𝒱ets can also test to see if your cat has worms. The types of worms that affect cats are roundworms, hookworms, and tapeworms. Weight loss is one of the most common warning signs in cats with worms. Other signs are white specks in your cat's poop or a sore on your cat. A vet will know how to treat your cat to get rid of worms or other diseases or parasites.

Cats also need shots to protect them from diseases. Vets provide information on the vaccines that your cat will need. Regular visits to the vet will usually keep your cat healthy.

A vet can also put a microchip under a cat's skin to identify the cat's owner. If your cat gets lost and is found by someone, a vet or the animal control central of your local police department will scan the microchip to see who owns the cat. Cats can also wear a collar with an identification tag to find their owners.

To keep your cat healthy, closely watch his behavior. Every cat has his own way of sending messages to people. Cats sometimes hide illnesses and injuries. Look for signs of hidden injuries, parasite infestation, or lumps. If you notice any signs that your cat is sick, take him to the vet as soon as possible. A healthy cat can have a long life.

NEUTERING OR SPAYING

Vets can do many things to keep your cat healthy. One thing is to spay girl cats and neuter boy cats. A neutered or spayed cat cannot make kittens. Cats can have a large number of kittens during their lifetime. Neutering or spaying not only helps control the population of cats but also reduces the risk of some cancers in cats. Good cat owners do everything possible to give their cats longer and healthier lives.

DECLAWING

Declawing is a surgery that permanently removes a cat's claws. Declawing provides no health benefit to a cat and is done strictly for human benefit. For example, some owners declaw their cats to keep them from climbing up curtains or scratching furniture.

If you decide to declaw your cat, have a certified vet perform this surgery. Your cat may have to stay at the veterinary hospital one to two days after surgery. It is best to declaw a cat before it is five months old. Kittens tend to recover quicker and adapt better to the loss of their claws. Because the back feet of a cat are not used as often for scratching, the front feet are usually the ones declawed. Most declawed cats will carry on normal activities, as well as carrying out scratching motion. Declawed cats should never be allowed outside, because they can no longer defend themselves.

> Declawing a cat is like cutting a human finger off at the knuckle, so some people believe that declawing cats is unnatural and cruel and can result in emotional damage to your cat.

POPULAR BREEDS OF CATS

There are many breeds, or kinds of pet cats. Choose a breed that fits your needs as an owner. The following are five of the most popular breeds:

Catwalk

Persian

Persian cats have long hair and short, broad bodies; short legs; and large heads. Their ears are small and their round faces are flat, with a small, flat nose. Persians are the most popular cat breed in the world. Persians come in a wide range of colors, including white, orange, gray, black, or even a mixture of these colors.

Persians are gentle and cuddly with soft, fluffy fur. Their fur may grow up to three inches long. Persians need to stay indoors. Their fine fur does not keep them warm in cold weather. A Persian's fur can clump and become matted, so Persians need to be combed every day. Persians are not energetic and will spend most of the day resting.

SIAMESE

Siamese cats have short hair and long, slim bodies. Their heads are triangle shaped with big, blue eyes and large, pointy ears. Siamese cats are also very popular. A Siamese cat can have fur that is light brown, silver, lilac, or white. Siamese have darker fur on their tails, ears, faces, and legs. These areas are called points. Siamese cats need a great deal of attention. They tend to make a lot of different sounds including meows and howls that sometimes sound like a crying baby. They are very active and energetic, and they love to play.

MAINE COON

Maine Coons come in many patterns and colors. They have long hair, large bodies with broad chests, and long, bushy tails. They have round eyes that are usually gold, copper, or green, and are one of the oldest natural breeds in North America. Maine Coons are named after Maine, their state of origin in America.

The most common is the brown tabby. Maine Coon's long fur needs to be groomed often so that it will not get matted. Maine Coons are easygoing and friendly. They are very strong and are good hunters. They are also very curious and like to play and climb.

RAGDOLL

Ragdolls have long hair and large, muscular bodies with a broad chest. Their heads are broad and triangle shaped. Ragdolls can be bi-color, pointed, or mitted. Bi-color ragdolls have an inverted "V" of white over their faces and chins, and their legs and tummies are also white. Pointed ragdolls have color on their heads, ears, legs, and tails. Mitted Ragdolls have little white "mitts" on their paws. Although Ragdolls have long hair, it does not mat much.

Ragdolls should be groomed about once a week. Ragdolls are gentle and friendly and like to be around people. Ragdolls are also quiet and do not meow often. Ragdolls are very active, energetic, and playful.

When you pick up a Ragdoll cat, most will go limp, like a ragdoll.

ABYSSINIAN

Abyssinians have short hair and slim, muscular bodies with long legs. They have a triangle-shaped head with gold or green almond-shaped eyes. Most Abyssinians are brownish red with black ticking. Ticking means each hair has a base color with three or four darker-colored bands. They are famous for their ticked fur.

Abyssinians are one of the oldest cat breeds. They love to climb and jump. They are also smart and curious and like attention. Abyssinians will follow their owners around the house, because they want to play. Abyssinians are quiet, gentle, and loving cats.

CONCLUSION

There are many types of pet cats, along with mixed breeds of no clear type. All cats needs plenty of love, care, and attention. With proper care, cats will most likely share their owner's life for ten or more years.

Cats are good company. They can be friendly and delight their owners. Stroke a cat, and it might even sound like it is talking to you. When a cat purrs, you know he is happy. Your cat's purr may help you feel relaxed and at ease, too.

GLOSSARY/INDEX

- **Animal Shelter** - a place that cares for animals that do not have homes

- **Breed** - to raise animals, such as cats, that have certain traits

- **Catnip** - an herb that excites cats

- **Checkup** - a routine examination by a doctor

- **Declawing** - permanently removing a cat's claws in a surgical procedure performed by a veterinarian while the cat is under anesthesia

- **Hairball** - a lump of hair that forms in a cat's stomach

- **Indoor** - not outside

- **Mammals** - warm-blooded animals that have backbones

- **Matted** - tangled into thick knots

- **Neutered** - when male cats have the organs removed that help them produce kittens

- **Spayed** - when female cats have the organs removed that help them produce kittens

- **Ticked** - each hair has a base color with three or four darker bands

- **Vaccination** - usually a shot that dispenses medications that prevent harmful diseases

- **Veterinarian (vet)** - a doctor who takes care of animals

WEBSITES

- www.aspca.org
- www.catsinternational.org
- kids.cfa.org
- factmonster.info/cats1.html

ABOUT THE AUTHORS

Andrea M. Nelson-Royes

Andrea M. Nelson-Royes, EdD, lives in the southeastern United States with her husband and four children. She is an educational researcher, and author of *Transforming Early Learners into Superb Readers: Promoting Literacy at School, at Home, and within the Community, Success in School and Career: Common Core Standards in Language Arts K–5,* and *Why Tutoring?: A Way to Achieve Success in School.* Her articles have appeared in the *Reading Improvement Journal* and *Illinois Schools Journal.* Nelson-Royes holds a doctoral degree in educational and organizational leadership from Nova Southeastern University in Florida. She can be contacted at:
Website: www.andreanelsonroyes.com
Twitter: @ANelsonRoyesEdD

Natalie A. Royes

Natalie A. Royes lives in the southeastern region of the United States with her family. Natalie is a student who loves to read, write, and do research. Natalie started writing as soon as she was able to read. She is an avid animal lover and has a cat named April and a dog named Kingston.

ILLUSTRATOR

Jerry Craft

Jerry craft has illustrated and / or written more than two dozen children's books, comic books, and board games. Most recent is a middle grade novel co-written with his two teenage sons, Jaylen and Aren called: "The Offenders: Saving The World While Serving Detention!" - an adventure story that teaches kids about the effects of bullying. He is the creator of Mama's Boyz, a comic strip that won four African American Literary Awards and was distributed by King Features from 1995-2013.

He also illustrated "The Zero Degree Zombie Zone," for Scholastic.
For more information, email him at: jerrycraft@aol.com or visit www.jerrycraft.net
Follow him on Twitter @JerryCraft

www.ingramcontent.com/pod-product-compliance
Lightning Source LLC
Chambersburg PA
CBHW041229040426
42444CB00002B/99